# Roger Williams

## Discover the Life of a Colonial American

Kieran Walsh

**Rourke**

Publishing LLC

Vero Beach, Florida 32964

www.rourkepublishing.com

PHOTO CREDITS: Pages 4, 10 ©Getty Images; Cover and page 7 used by permission of The Christian Hall of Fame, Canton Baptist Temple, Canton, Ohio; all other photos ©North Wind Picture Archives

Title Page: *Roger Williams lands in America for the first time.*

Editor: Frank Sloan

Cover and page design by Nicola Stratford

**Library of Congress Cataloging-in-Publication Data**

Walsh, Kieran.
  Roger Williams / Kieran Walsh.
    p. cm. -- (Discover the life of a colonial American)
  Includes bibliographical references and index.
  ISBN 1-59515-140-0
  1. Williams, Roger, 1604?-1683--Juvenile literature. 2. Puritans--Rhode Island--Biography--Juvenile literature. 3. Pioneers--Rhode Island--Biography--Juvenile literature. 4. Baptists--Rhode Island--Biography--Juvenile literature. 5. Separatists--Rhode Island--Biography--Juvenile literature. 6. Rhode Island--History--Colonial period, ca. 1600-1775--Juvenile literature. I. Title. II. Series: Walsh, Kieran. Discover the life of a colonial American.
  F82.W7W55 2004
  974.5'02'092--dc22

2004009657

Printed in the USA

CG/CG

# Table of Contents

# The Young Williams

Roger Williams was born in 1603 in England. He grew up in a section of London called Holborn, near where **heretics** had been burned at the stake in the 16th century.

When he was a teenager, Williams's writing skills attracted the attention of Sir Edward Coke, a judge. In 1621, Coke arranged for Williams to attend Sutton's Hospital, a school now called Charterhouse School. After this, Williams went on to Cambridge University where he studied law and theology.

*Roger Williams as a young man*

# Priesthood

Williams became an **Anglican** priest in 1627. But while serving as the **chaplain** to a wealthy family in Essex, Williams realized that his own religious beliefs were very different from the Church of England's.

Among other things, Williams believed that people should be allowed to worship God in their own ways. He also believed that religion and **government** should be kept separate.

*Roger Williams as a priest*

# America

In 1631, Williams moved to America and settled in the colony of Massachusetts. For a time, he worked as a teacher and eventually became a minister in Salem.

Even in America, Williams found that his ideas were too **radical** for his fellow colonists.

*Williams meets with friendly Native Americans in the 1630s.*

**Williams believed** strongly that the colonists should deal fairly with Native Americans. He also believed that the colonists should break completely with the Church of England.

*Williams and his family were forced to leave Massachusetts.*

# Forced to Leave

Williams's views were so unpopular that he was put on trial. Although he was nearly deported, Williams was instead forced to leave Massachusetts as punishment.

# Rhode Island

Traveling south, Williams purchased some land from a Native American tribe called the

**Narragansett**. This land would become the **colony** of Providence in 1636.

*Williams fled south to what would become Providence.*

*Williams often met with Native Americans.*

# New Settlers

Williams wanted the colony of Providence to allow religious **tolerance**. In the years that followed, Providence filled with people from Europe and even other American colonies who were fleeing religious **persecution**. These groups included Baptists, Quakers, Jews, and Calvinists.

*Williams built a new home for his family in Providence.*

# The Patent

By 1643, the population of Providence had spread outward. Neighboring towns were established, including Portsmouth, Providence, Newport, and Warwick.

In 1643, Williams journeyed to England to get a **patent** that would join all these towns together as one colony—Rhode Island.

**When this** patent was challenged in 1651, Williams returned to England to have the patent restored.

*Williams returned from England with a charter to create Rhode Island.*

In 1675, tensions between the Native Americans and the colonists led to King Philip's War. During this war, nearly all of Providence was burned down.

*A scene showing a battle in King Philip's War*

# President of the Colony

Beginning in 1654, Williams served as the president of the Rhode Island colony. He would eventually serve three terms.

*Williams had friendly dealings with Native Americans.*

# Rhode Island

Fortunately, Williams lived to see most of Providence rebuilt. In the last years of his life, he also saw Rhode Island becoming an important center of trade and industry.

Williams continued preaching until his death in 1683. His vision of a world of tolerance and respect lives on in Rhode Island.

*Roger Williams is remembered as the founder of Rhode Island.*

# Important Dates to Remember

| | |
|---|---|
| 1603 | Born in England |
| 1621 | Attends Sutton's Hospital |
| 1627 | Becomes an Anglican priest |
| 1631 | Moves to America and settles in the colony of Massachusetts |
| 1636 | Founds colony of Rhode Island |
| 1643 | Returns to England to get a patent for the colony of Rhode Island |
| 1654 | Serves first of three terms as president of Rhode Island colony |
| 1675 | King Philip's War; much of Providence is burned |
| 1683 | Dies in Rhode Island |

# Glossary

**Anglican** (AN gli kun) — part of the Church of England

**chaplain** (CHAP lun) — a clergyman who is connected to a wealthy household

**colony** (KOL un ee) — a group of people who settle far from home but maintain ties to their homeland.

**government** (GUV ern munt) — the ruling body of a country

**heretics** (HAIR uh tiks) — people who disagree with established religious teachings

**Narragansett** (NAR uh GAN sut) — a Native American tribe of Rhode Island

**patent** (PAT unt) — an agreement; a contract

**persecution** (PUR sih kyu shun) — mistreatment

**radical** (RAD uh kul) — very different from established beliefs

**tolerance** (TOL ur ents) — respect, understanding

# Index

## Further Reading

Avi. *Finding Providence: The Story of Roger Williams*. Bt Bound, 1999
Kling, Andrew A. *The Thirteen Colonies: Rhode Island*. Lucent, 2001
Stefoff, Rebecca. *Colonial Times: 1600-1700*. Benchmark Books, 2001
Stefoff, Rebecca. *Voices from Colonial Life*. Benchmark Books, 2003

## Websites to Visit

http://www.infoplease.com/ce6/people/A0852336.html
Infoplease – Roger Williams
http://www.usahistory.info/New-England/Rhode-Island.html
History of the U.S.A. – Rhode Island and Providence Plantation
http://www.state.ri.us/
Rhode Island Online

## About the Author

Kieran Walsh is a writer of children's nonfiction books, primarily on historical and social studies topics. Walsh has been involved in the children's book field as editor, proofreader, and illustrator as well as author.